BIBLE 401
HOW CAN I LIVE FOR GOD?

Author:
Emma Jean Clark, M.Ed.

Editor:
Richard W. Wheeler, M.A. Ed.

Consulting Editor:
John L. Booth, Th.D.

Revision Editor:
Alan Christopherson, M.S.

Media Credits:
Page 3: © Jani Bryson, iStock, Thinkstock; **4:** © William Perry, Hemera, Thinkstock; **6:** © ZvonimirAtleti, iStock, Thinkstock; **7:** © Jaroslaw Baczewski, iStock, Thinkstock; **10:** © Peter Dennis, Dorling Kindersley, Thinkstock; **13:** © Dorling Kindersley, Thinkstock; **15:** © Leong Kin Fei, iStock, Thinkstock **17:** © Yuran, iStock, Thinkstock; **18:** © Dorling Kindersley, iStock, Thinkstock **27:** © David De Lossy, Photodisk, Thinkstock; **28:** © Dorling Kindersley, Thinkstock; **32:** © artisitcco, iStock, Thinkstock; **37:** © Peter Dennis, Dorling Kindersley, Thinkstock; **39:** © colematt, iStock, Thinkstock.

Alpha Omega
PUBLICATIONS

804 N. 2nd Ave. E.
Rock Rapids, IA 51246-1759

HOW CAN I LIVE FOR GOD?

While studying this LIFEPAC®, you will learn more about how you can live for God. To help you live for Him, God has provided you with a new life in Christ. Before Jesus went back to heaven, He promised to send the Holy Spirit. You first come to know God as He speaks to you from His Word. Then you have the opportunity of daily living with Christ because the Holy Spirit is your helper. As you live in obedience to the Word of God, others will notice your new life, the Christ-life in you. God will provide occasions for you to explain to others how they can receive Christ.

In this LIFEPAC you will study how Peter, one of Christ's first followers, lived for God and how you can also live for God.

Objectives

Read these objectives. The objectives tell you what you will be able to do when you have successfully completed this LIFEPAC. Each section will list according to the numbers below what objectives will be met in that section. When you have finished this LIFEPAC, you should be able to:

1. Tell how Peter found Jesus.
2. List the results of Peter's Pentecost sermon.
3. Repeat what Jesus asked Peter to do after Jesus arose from the dead.
4. Tell how Peter lived for God.
5. Explain how a person is born again.
6. Explain how a Christian grows.
7. Tell how you can live for God.

1. HOW PETER LIVED FOR GOD

After Peter came to Jesus Christ, he answered Jesus' call to follow Him. After a period of training, Peter "fished for men" and "fed God's sheep."

Objectives

Review these objectives. When you have completed this section, you should be able to:

1. Tell how Peter found Jesus.
2. List the results of Peter's Pentecost sermon.
3. Repeat what Jesus asked Peter to do after Jesus arose from the dead.
4. Tell how Peter lived for God.

Vocabulary

Study these new words. Learning the meanings of these words is a good study habit and will improve your understanding of this LIFEPAC.

basin (bā′ sn). Bowl.

Bethsaida (beth′ sā′ i du). Peter's home town.

career (ku rir′). The work a person chooses to do through his working years.

debt (det). That which is owed to another.

diary (dī′ ur ē). A written record of what you do each day.

disciple (du sī′ pul). A person who follows and believes in a leader and his teachings.

faith (fāth). Belief or trust.

forgive (fur giv′). Not have hard feelings toward.

foundation (foun dā′ shun). The part that other parts rest on for support.

grader (grā′ dur). A person who is in a certain grade at school.

interview (in' tur vyü). A meeting to talk over something special.

obedience (ō bē' dē uns). The act of obeying.

Pentecost (pen' tu kôst). Feast of Weeks that came fifty days after Passover.

pray (prā). To talk to God.

preach (prē ch). To give a sermon.

repent (ri pent'). To change from going your own way to going God's way.

salary (sal' ur ē). A certain amount of money that is paid to someone for work that he does.

sandal (san' dl). A shoe with a sole that is fastened to the foot by a strap or straps.

sin (sin). Doing wrong.

Note: *All vocabulary words in this LIFEPAC appear in* **boldface** *print the first time they are used. If you are unsure of the meaning when you are reading, study the definitions given.*

Pronunciation Key: hat, āge, cāre, fär; let, ēqual, tėrm; it, īce; hot, ōpen, ôrder; oil; out; cup, pùt, rüle; child; long; thin; /ŦH/ for then; /zh/ for measure; /u/ or /ə/ represents /a/ in about, /e/ in taken, /i/ in pencil, /o/ in lemon, and /u/ in circus.

Peter Found Jesus

 Read John 1:28-44.

The twins, Leonard and Linda, are fourth **graders**. Their class is learning about different **careers**. Each student has chosen one career that interests him. Linda and Leonard have been learning about their uncle's work in Israel. Today Linda is giving her report. You are invited to listen to it.

"I have been interested in what my uncle is doing in Israel. His work is finding out what happened in the past. He does this work by digging into the earth and looking for objects. He has also learned to read Hebrew. My uncle wanted to be able to read any writing that he found. I was very excited about his letter. I thought you might like to hear part of it. I brought it to read to you."

Linda's uncle wrote, "We have been digging near the shores of the Sea of Galilee. The village of **Bethsaida**, where Peter lived, stood here. Now the old village is broken down and covered with earth. We dig to find broken bricks, tiles, coins, and lamps.

| Bethesda. Old City, Jerusalem

We use different tests on them to find out how old they are. When we had dug deep enough, we found many things that were as old as the time of Christ. The **foundation** stones of two houses were found.

"I thought it might make our work more interesting to you if I pretended that one of the houses belonged to Peter and his wife and the other house to friends of Peter's. Let's pretend that the little girl in the house next to Peter's kept a **diary.** We will call the little girl *Hali*. I will write to you what I think Hali might have written in her diary. Her diary might have been written on a scroll." Many people wrote on scrolls in Jesus' day. Hali might have written her diary like the following page.

Wednesday — Today I was looking out of the window. The house next door belongs to Simon, son of Jona. Simon's brother, Andrew, came to the house while I was looking. I heard Andrew tell Simon why he had come. He wanted Simon to meet a man called Jesus.

| John the Baptist

Andrew has been a **disciple** of John the Baptist. Well, a few days ago, this man they call *Jesus* came to the place where John and two of his disciples were. One of these disciples was Andrew. John introduced Jesus as the *Lamb of God, which taketh away the* **sin** *of the world.* I wonder why John called Jesus *the Lamb of God?* It must have something to do with the lambs we kill. The lambs are sacrificed for our sin. Will Jesus also die for our sin? Simon went with his brother, Andrew, to see Jesus. I hope Simon will tell me about it when he comes back.

"That was what my uncle wrote for Hali's diary on the first day. Here is how Hali's diary read a few days later."

I heard Simon when he came back home. He was so excited. I could hear him tell his family what happened. Jesus had called him by his name, Simon, son of Jona. Jesus even knew who Simon's father was! Would Jesus know my name? Would Jesus know who my parents are? I'd like to meet Jesus. Simon said that Jesus gave him a new name, Peter. Peter means a *stone*. I wonder why Jesus gave Peter a new name meaning a *stone?* Maybe some day I'll know. Would Jesus give me a new name? What would it mean?

That's all the news for today. Isn't it exciting? How can I ever sleep?"

"That's Hali's diary for the first few days. That's all I have for my report," Linda said.

Everyone was interested in Linda's report. They were all interested in what her uncle would write for the rest of the diary. The teacher said that Linda could read the rest of it to the class.

That evening Linda made a puzzle for her class to work. Here is one for you on the following page.

Complete this activity to discover a very important message.

1.1 Fill in the lines after the clues. Some lines have numbers under them. In the last step (j.), write the letters on the lines above the same number. If you do it right, you'll read a most important message.

a. What did John call Jesus? _____ _____ _____ _____
                                        7

   _____ _____   _____ _____ _____

b. How many disciples were with John? _____ _____ _____
                                          6   12

c. What did these disciples do?

   _____ _____ _____ _____   _____ _____ _____
                                        2

   _____ _____ _____ _____ _____
    1   9   15

d. Which disciple had a brother? _____ _____ _____ _____ _____ _____
                                    11   17

e. What was his brother's name?_____ _____ _____ _____ _____
                                  3   16

   _____ _____ _____ _____ _____

f. What did Andrew do? _____ _____ _____ _____ _____ _____ _____

   _____ _____ _____ _____   _____ _____

   _____ _____ _____ _____ _____
                    4

g. What did Jesus do? _____ _____ _____ _____

   _____ _____ _____ _____   _____

   _____ _____ _____   _____ _____ _____
                    13

h. What did Peter's new name mean?

   _____ _____ _____ _____ _____ _____
        10

i. What did John say Jesus would do? _____ _____ _____ _____
                                                          8

   _____ _____ _____ _____   _____ _____ _____ _____
              14   5

j. _____ _____ _____ _____ _____   _____ _____ _____ _____ _____
    1   2   3   4   5   6   7   8   9   10

   _____ _____ _____ _____   _____ _____ _____
   11   12   13   14   15   16   17

Do this map activity.

1.2   On the map of New Testament Israel, find the city, Bethsaida, where Peter lived (John 1:44). Circle the name of the city on the map.

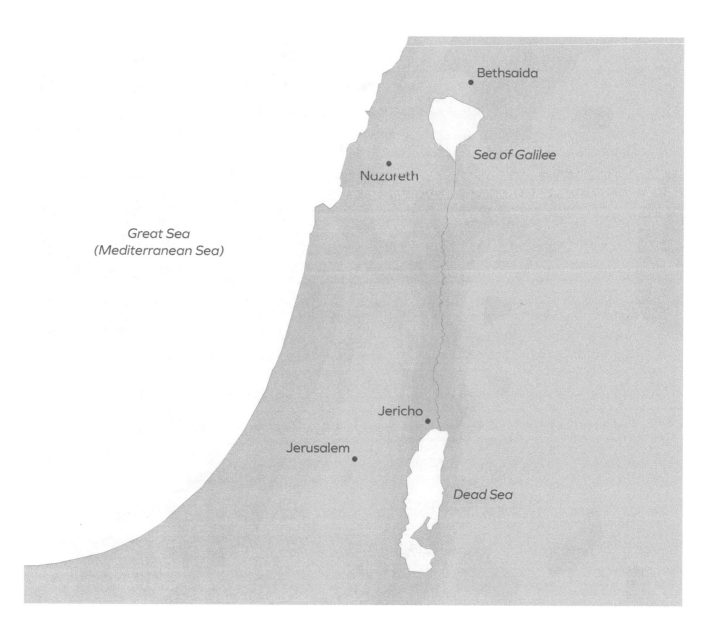

Peter Followed Jesus

 Read Matthew 4:18–20.

The next few letters that Linda received from her uncle contained more pages from Hali's diary. The letters described the things that Peter learned from Jesus. The first letter said,

 Today I went walking by the Sea of Galilee. Simon Peter and Andrew were fishing. Jesus walked by. I was so excited. I listened to Him talk to the men. Jesus told them if they would follow Him, they could fish for men. I was really surprised when they stopped fishing. I wonder what *fishing for men* means?

Peter's obedience. From Hali's diary:

I wonder what my father would have done if Jesus had asked him to give up his job and follow Jesus. I didn't hear Jesus say anything about **salary**. I wonder how Simon Peter will get food and clothes. Peter obeyed Jesus. I think he had **faith** in Jesus.

I asked Simon Peter why he would give up his job to follow Jesus. He told me that he believed Jesus was God's Son and the Savior of the world. Everyone should obey God's Son.

| Disciples Simon, Andrew, James, and John pulling a catch of fish to a boat

Interview two adults who work. Ask them what they would do if they were offered a new job by a stranger.

1.3   Name of first person interviewed. a. _____

Write their answer to your question here. b. _____

_____

1.4   Name of second person interviewed. a. _____

Write their answer to your question here. b. _____

_____

Write a letter to Hali.

1.5   Tell Hali why you think Peter followed Jesus.
Tell her whether you think Peter was right or wrong.
Explain why you think as you do.

_____

Date

Dear Hali,

_____

_____

_____

_____

_____ ,

_____

Teacher check:

Initials _____   Date _____

Read a book and write a book report.

1.6 Choose a book about someone in the twentieth century who followed Jesus. Your teacher or your parents can help you find a book. Share your book report with them when you have finished it.

Title of the book _____

Author _____

1.7 Did you like the book?   Yes   No   (Circle your answer.)

1.8 Answer one of the following questions.
a. What did you like about the book?
b. What didn't you like about the book?

_____

_____

_____

_____

_____

_____

_____

Stop

✓ **Teacher check:**

Initials _____   Date _____

Peter's faith. In the next letter Linda's uncle sent more from Hali's diary.

Read Matthew 14:22–33.

Peter was home. I got to hear about his latest adventure with Jesus. Yesterday many people came to hear Jesus. Only one boy brought something to eat. When it was getting late, Jesus told His disciples to feed the people. All the food they could find was the boy's lunch. Jesus used the lunch to feed over five thousand people. I wish I could have been there.

After that, Jesus told the disciples to take the boat to the other side of the lake. Then Jesus went up into a mountain to **pray**. When the boat was halfway across, the wind began to blow. The disciples in the boat saw someone walking on the water. They couldn't tell who it was. All the disciples were afraid. Jesus told them who He was. He told them not to be afraid. Peter wanted to walk on the water. Jesus told him to come. Peter did walk on water, but the wind was blowing hard, and the waves were high. Peter began to look around. He looked at the waves. He became afraid. He took his eyes off
of Jesus and he started to sink. Peter called to Jesus to rescue him. Jesus took Peter's hand and asked him why he had doubted. Jesus and Peter got in the boat. The wind stopped blowing. Then the disciples all said that Jesus was God's Son.

| Jesus walking on water

Do this puzzle.

1.9 Linda was interested in the names of the twelve disciples. She found their names in Matthew 10:1 –10:4. She made a puzzle for her class. See if you can find the names of the disciples. Look down and across. Put a ring around their names. Write their names on the lines following the puzzle.

Z	A	C	C	H	E	U	J	E	S	S	E	N
A	D	A	M	A	R	D	U	N	B	P	N	A
C	A	D	A	T	H	A	D	D	A	E	U	S
H	N	O	B	H	E	V	A	A	R	T	M	O
A	I	N	A	E	R	I	S	A	T	E	O	L
R	E	I	R	O	O	D	I	D	H	R	S	O
I	M	A	T	T	H	E	W	J	O	S	E	M
A	O	R	I	H	E	R	O	D	L	A	S	O
S	S	C	M	O	R	J	A	C	O	B	A	N
I	E	J	A	M	E	S	A	I	M	A	T	A
A	P	A	R	A	B	A	T	T	E	S	A	I
N	H	C	C	S	I	M	W	O	W	I	L	L
D	I	S	C	I	P	L	E	S	A	I	A	S
R	L	J	A	M	E	S	L	I	S	A	I	I
E	I	O	J	O	H	N	V	M	O	S	E	M
W	P	N	O	N	A	A	E	E	N	O	C	E

a. _____   b. _____

c. _____   d. _____

e. _____   f. _____

g. _____   h. _____

i. _____   j. _____

k. _____   l. _____

Peter's question. Several weeks passed before a letter came from Linda's Uncle Gerald. He had written more of Hali's diary for Linda. Listen to this part:

Read Matthew 18:21–35.

Today I was very upset with my friend. She tore my doll's dress. I told her to go home. I didn't want to ever see her again. She left, but I felt so bad, I began to cry. My neighbor, Simon Peter, came along. He asked me what was wrong. I told him all about it. I asked him if I had to **forgive** her. He told me about asking Jesus a question something like that. He said he asked Jesus how many times he had to forgive someone. Peter suggested seven times. Jesus told Peter not seven times but seventy times seven.

I bent down to multiply that in the sand – 490 times! How would I ever keep track of how many times I had already forgiven her?

While I was thinking, Peter told me a story. It was the story Jesus told him. It was about a man who owed a king a lot of money. The man didn't have the money to pay his **debt**. The king was going to sell the man and his family. The man begged the king for more time. He promised to pay. The king forgave the man.

This man who had been forgiven by the king met a man who owed him a smaller amount of money. The first man demanded the money at once. The other man begged for more time. He promised to pay. The forgiven man would not give the other man more time. He had him put in prison. The king heard what the forgiven man had done. The king was angry and had that man punished.

This story reminded Peter of what Jesus had taught his disciples to pray. When I heard what Jesus had taught his disciples to pray, I decided to forgive my friend.

| Jesus forgiving

Do this puzzle.

1.10 Linda found the verse in her Bible. She wrote it in code for her classmates. Can you figure it out? Using the Number Code Key, write the correct letters on the lines above the numbers.

Number Code

1 = A	5 = E	9 = I	13 = M	17 = Q	21 = U	25= Y
2 = B	6 = F	10 = J	14 = N	18 = R	22 = V	26= Z
3 = C	7 = G	11 = K	15 = O	19 = S	23 = W	
4 = D	8 = H	12 = L	16 = P	20 = T	24 = X	

‾1‾ ‾14‾ ‾4‾   ‾6‾ ‾15‾ ‾18‾ ‾7‾ ‾9‾ ‾22‾ ‾5‾   ‾21‾ ‾19‾   ‾15‾ ‾21‾ ‾18‾

‾4‾ ‾5‾ ‾2‾ ‾20‾ ‾19‾   ‾1‾ ‾19‾   ‾23‾ ‾5‾

‾6‾ ‾15‾ ‾18‾ ‾7‾ ‾9‾ ‾22‾ ‾5‾   ‾15‾ ‾21‾ ‾18‾

‾4‾ ‾5‾ ‾2‾ ‾20‾ ‾15‾ ‾18‾ ‾19‾   ‾13‾ ‾1‾ ‾20‾ ‾20‾ ‾8‾ ‾5‾ ‾23‾   6:12

Jesus' teaching. The next letter from Uncle Gerald had more from Hali's diary.

One entry stated,

 **Read John 13:4-11.**

 I had a letter from Peter today. He said, "Dear Friend, Jesus taught me a lesson. I thought it might help you. Two nights ago, after we had eaten, Jesus poured water into a **basin**. He began to wash our feet. At first, I wouldn't let Him wash my feet. Then Jesus said I couldn't be His follower if He didn't wash my feet. So then I wanted Him to wash me all over. But Jesus said we only needed to be washed all over *once*. He said we only need to have our feet washed again."

"Jesus was teaching a lesson by using an example. You take a bath. Then you go out to play. Sand gets in your **sandals**. When you pull them off at night your feet are dirty. You need to wash your feet before you go to bed."

"Our hearts need the same kind of cleansing each day. Jesus cleansed our hearts when he took away our sin, but sometimes we don't obey God. Sometimes we don't have faith. We don't forgive someone. When this happens, we need to have our hearts cleansed from these things."

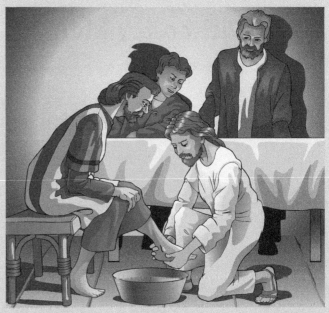

| Our hearts need daily cleansing, too.

"I know that Jesus forgave my sins and made my heart clean. I also know I need to have my life cleansed every day, too."

"But, dear Hali, that was the last meal we had with Jesus. The soldiers took Jesus away and killed Him. I will write to you again soon, but I find it too hard to talk about now."

I can't talk about it, either.

Write the letter on the line to match these items.

1.11 _____ number of people Jesus fed

1.12 _____ number of disciples

1.13 _____ number of times Peter thought you should forgive

1.14 _____ number of times Jesus said you should forgive

a. 7

b. 12

c. 490

d. 5,000+

e. 4,500

Peter Fished for Men

 **Read Acts 2:14–41.**

When Linda came from school, she found a letter from Uncle Gerald. She read, "Dear Leonard and Linda, I've come to the place in Hali's diary of events that took place after Jesus' death."

Here is part of Hali's diary that Uncle Gerald wrote for the children.

My friend's family made the pilgrimage to Jerusalem last week for the Feast of Weeks. The Feast of Weeks is also called **Pentecost** because it is just fifty days after the barley offering during Passover. That was just fifty days after Jesus arose from the dead. We all felt so sad when we heard that Jesus had been killed. Peter says he knows Jesus arose from the dead. Peter says that he saw Jesus several times afterwards.

My friend's family heard Peter **preach** while they were in Jerusalem. My friend said it was so exciting! First, the Holy Spirit of God filled the disciples and followers of Christ. They were able to preach in the languages of all the foreign visitors. In that one day three thousand people believed what Peter told them about Jesus. Peter told them that they should **repent** and be baptized. They took Jesus as their Savior and were baptized.

Everybody is talking about it—even in Bethsaida. They say more people keep repenting and taking Jesus as their Savior every day.

Do these activities.

Use the Morse code to figure out the message from the Bible.

International Morse Code

A	• ▬	K	▬ • ▬	U	• • ▬	5	• • • • •
B	▬ • • •	L	• ▬ • •	V	• • • ▬	6	▬ • • • •
C	▬ • ▬ •	M	▬ ▬	W	• ▬ ▬	7	▬ ▬ • • •
D	▬ • •	N	▬ •	X	▬ • • ▬	8	▬ ▬ ▬ • •
E	•	O	▬ ▬ ▬	Y	▬ • ▬ ▬	9	▬ ▬ ▬ ▬ •
F	• • ▬ •	P	• ▬ ▬ •	Z	▬ ▬ • •	0	▬ ▬ ▬ ▬ ▬
G	▬ ▬ •	Q	▬ ▬ • ▬	1	• ▬ ▬ ▬ ▬	Comma	• ▬ • ▬ • ▬
H	• • • •	R	• ▬ •	2	• • ▬ ▬ ▬	Colon	▬ ▬ ▬ • • •
I	• •	S	• • •	3	• • • ▬ ▬	Quotation	
J	• ▬ ▬ ▬	T	▬	4	• • • • ▬	marks	• ▬ • • ▬ •

1.15 Linda took part of Peter's message and wrote it in Morse code. See if you can figure out the message. Write the letters in the lines above the Morse code signs.

International Morse Code

A	● ▬	K	▬ ● ▬	U	● ● ▬	5	● ● ● ● ●
B	▬ ● ● ●	L	● ▬ ● ●	V	● ● ● ▬	6	▬ ● ● ● ●
C	▬ ● ▬ ●	M	▬ ▬	W	● ▬ ▬	7	▬ ▬ ● ● ●
D	▬ ● ●	N	▬ ●	X	▬ ● ● ▬	8	▬ ▬ ▬ ● ●
E	●	O	▬ ▬ ▬	Y	▬ ● ▬ ▬	9	▬ ▬ ▬ ▬ ●
F	● ● ▬ ●	P	● ▬ ▬ ●	Z	▬ ▬ ● ●	0	▬ ▬ ▬ ▬ ▬
G	▬ ▬ ●	Q	▬ ▬ ● ▬	1	● ▬ ▬ ▬ ▬	Comma	● ▬ ● ▬ ● ▬
H	● ● ● ●	R	● ▬ ●	2	● ● ▬ ▬ ▬	Colon	▬ ▬ ▬ ● ● ●
I	● ●	S	● ● ●	3	● ● ● ▬ ▬	Quotation	
J	● ▬ ▬ ▬	T	▬	4	● ● ● ● ▬	marks	● ▬ ● ● ▬ ●

▬ ▬ ▬ ▬
● ▬ ● ● ▬ ▬ ▬ ● ▬ ● ● ▬ ▬ ●

▬ ▬ ▬ ▬ ▬
● ● ● ● ● ● ● ▬ ● ▬ ● ● ● ▬ ● ●

▬ ▬ ▬ ▬ ▬ ▬ ● ▬ ● ▬
▬ ● ● ● ▬ ● ● ● ● ▬ ● ● ● ● ● ▬ ● ● ● ▬ ● ● ● ●

▬ ▬ ▬ ▬ : ▬ ▬ ▬ ▬
● ▬ ● ▬ ● ▬ ● ▬ ● ● ● ▬ ▬ ● ● ● ● ▬ ● ▬ ▬ ●

1.16 Write the Bible verse, Acts 2:21, on these lines.

_____

_____

_____

Memorize Acts 2:21.

Say it from memory to a teacher.

1.17 Write a newspaper story on events in Peter's life following his

Teacher check:

Initials _____

Date _____

first sermon.

Base your story on an event recorded in Acts chapter 3 or 4. Pretend you are a reporter for a newspaper, *The Jerusalem Journal*.

Write as if you were living in Peter's time.

_____

(HEADLINE)

_____
_____
_____
_____
_____
_____
_____
_____

Teacher check:

Initials _____ Date _____

Peter Fed Sheep

 Read John 21:15–17.

When the next letter came from Uncle Gerald, it had good news. He was coming back to the United States for a visit. He would be able to answer all the questions the family had about his work.

He also sent some more of Hali's diary. Hali told about a letter from Peter.

Today our family received a letter from our neighbor Peter. He told us why he was spending all of his time preaching. He said that after Jesus arose from the dead, seven of the disciples had gone fishing. They couldn't catch any fish. Later Jesus came and told them where to catch fish. They caught one hundred fifty-three! Then they ate breakfast with Jesus.

Here is the rest of Peter's letter:

"After breakfast Jesus asked me if I loved Him more than I loved the fishing business. He asked me the same question three times. He told me to feed His lambs and sheep and be a shepherd to His people."

"One way God wants me to feed His lambs and sheep is to take God's message to them."

"You are one of God's lambs. His message is that Jesus came to take away your sin. He died for your sins. You can be one of Jesus' lambs if you ask Jesus to be your Savior. You can follow Jesus. You can talk to Jesus. You can fish for boys and girls. Why don't you talk to God now? Tell Him about your sins. Tell Him you believe He died for your sins. Thank Him for dying for your sins. The Holy Spirit will live in your life, just as He has lived in mine since Pentecost."

"Write and let me know how things are going. Ask me any questions you have. I want to help you live for Jesus."

Peter

I have prayed to God and asked Him to let Jesus be my Savior. I don't understand it very well. I will learn more about it from my mother—from Peter, too, when he comes back to Bethsaida.

BIBLE 401

LIFEPAC TEST

NAME _____

DATE _____

SCORE _____

BIBLE 401: LIFEPAC TEST

Match these items (each answer counts 2 points).

1. _____ number of men Jesus trained
2. _____ number of times Peter thought you should forgive
3. _____ number of times Jesus said you should forgive
4. _____ number of people who repented when Peter preached
5. _____ number of times Jesus asked Peter the same question
6. _____ you can be born how many times
7. _____ names of the fruit of the Spirit
8. _____ number of people one girl brought to Jesus
9. _____ number of people God wants to perish
10. _____ number of people you can make sure live for God

a. 0
b. 1
c. 2
d. 3
e. 7
f. 9
g. 12
h. 29
i. 490
j. 3,000

Answer true or false (each answer counts 2 points).

11. _____ John introduced Jesus as the Lion of God.
12. _____ Jesus would take away the sin of the world.
13. _____ Peter's brother brought him to Jesus.
14. _____ Jesus wanted Peter to fish for fish.
15. _____ Jesus trained ten men.
16. _____ Jesus washed the disciples' faces.
17. _____ When Peter preached, many repented and took Jesus in their hearts.
18. _____ Jesus wanted Peter to feed His lambs.
19. _____ Peter's home town was Bethsaida.
20. _____ Peter asked Jesus about forgiveness.

Complete these items (each answer counts 4 points).

21. A disciple is _____ .

22. Sin is _____ .

23. Peter started to sink when _____ .

24. Every sinful heart needs to be _____ .

25. Nicodemus was a _____ .

26. God wants us to be _____ of His Word.

27. When we sin we should _____ it to God.

28. God will _____ our sin.

29. If we _____ for others, they will come to Jesus.

30. God wants _____ to repent and ask Jesus into their hearts.

Write the correct letter and answer on the blank (each answer counts 3 points).

31. If we only hear God's Word we _____ ourselves.
    a. deceive   b. deny   c. desire   d. defy

32. Peter asked Jesus a question about _____ .
    a. covetousness   b. faithfulness c. forgiveness   d. righteousness

33. Jesus told a story about a man who _____ .
    a. borrowed   b. owed   c. owned   d. stole

34. If we forgive others, Jesus will _____ us.
    a. fail   b. find   c. forgive   d. forsake

35. Others will come to Jesus if we _____ .
    a. beg   b. pray   c. preach   d. push

Do these activities (each answer counts 1 point).

36. Write four names of the fruit of the Spirit that were studied in this LIFEPAC.

    a. _____   b. _____

    c. _____   d. _____

BIB 401 LIFEPAC TEST

37. Write where the verse is found in the Bible that lists the names of the fruit of the

Spirit. _____

_____

Do this puzzle.

1.18   Read the puzzle clues and fill in the blanks.
Then write the words in the puzzle.

Across

1.   John called Jesus the _____ _____ _____ _____ of God.

4.   Peter's home town was

_____ _____ _____ _____ _____ _____ _____ _____ _____ .

6.   Jesus promised Peter he could fish for _____ _____ _____ .

Down

2.   Simon Peter's brother was named _____ _____ _____ _____ _____ _____ .

3.   Peter asked Jesus about

_____ _____ _____ _____ _____ _____ _____ _____ _____ _____ .

5.   John said Jesus would take away _____ _____ _____ .

Practice dividing words into syllables.

1.19 Remember that if two consonants come right after the first vowel in a word, the word is usually divided into syllables between the two consonants.

Example: cam / pus

Divide the words into syllables.

Word	First Syllable	Second Syllable
a. fountain	a. _____	b. _____
b. quarter	a. _____	b. _____
c. window	a. _____	b. _____
d. Linda	a. _____	b. _____
e. forgive	a. _____	b. _____
f. after	a. _____	b. _____
g. sandal	a. _____	b. _____
h. follow	a. _____	b. _____

1.20 Remember, when a word is divided into syllables, two consonants that make one sound, such as *sh, th, ch, wh*, are never separated.

Word	First Syllable	Second Syllable
a. worship	a. _____	b. _____
b. touching	a. _____	b. _____
c. truthful	a. _____	b. _____
d. meanwhile	a. _____	b. _____
e. breathless	a. _____	b. _____
f. although	a. _____	b. _____
g. nowhere	a. _____	b. _____

Review the material in this section to prepare for the Self Test. The Self Test will check your understanding of this section. Any items you miss on this test will show you what areas you will need to restudy in order to prepare for the unit test.

SELF TEST 1

Complete these statements (each answer counts 3 points).

1.01   Bethsaida was _____ .

1.02   A disciple is _____ .

1.03   A scroll is _____ .

1.04   Sin is _____ .

1.05   John introduced Jesus as _____ .

1.06   John said Jesus would _____ .

1.07   Simon Peter's brother was named _____ .

1.08   Jesus gave Peter a _____ .

1.09   Peter's new name meant _____ .

1.010   Jesus told Peter he could fish for _____ .

1.011   Peter questioned Jesus about _____ .

1.012   Peter didn't want Jesus to _____ .

1.013   When Peter preached, many people _____ .

1.014   After Jesus arose, He told Peter to _____ .

1.015   Jesus asked Peter one question _____ times.

Complete these activities (each numbered item counts 5 points).

1.016   When did Peter start to sink in the water? _____

_____

1.017   Tell the story Jesus told Peter about forgiveness.

_____

_____

_____

_____

1.018   What does this story in 1.017 teach you? _____

_____

1.019   How many responded to Peter's first sermon? _____

1.020   List four ways in which Peter lived for Jesus.

1. _____

2. _____

3. _____

4. _____

Divide the following words into syllables (each answer counts 2 points).

Word	First Syllable	Second Syllable
1.021 forgive	_____	_____
1.022 worship	_____	_____
1.023 sandal	_____	_____
1.024 truthful	_____	_____
1.025 after	_____	_____
1.026 wonder	_____	_____
1.027 follow	_____	_____
1.028 meanwhile	_____	_____
1.029 breathless	_____	_____
1.030 although	_____	_____
1.031 fifty	_____	_____
1.032 window	_____	_____
1.033 sermon	_____	_____
1.034 question	_____	_____
1.035 person	_____	_____

Teacher check: Initials _____

Score _____   Date _____

80 / 100

2. HOW I CAN LIVE FOR GOD

You have studied how Peter lived for God.

In this section you will study how you can live for God. You will study how to begin the Christian life. You will learn how to grow as a Christian. You will learn how the Holy Spirit wants you to live.

Objectives

Review these objectives. When you have completed this section, you should be able to:

5. Explain how a person is born again.
6. Explain how a Christian grows.
7. Tell how you can live for God.

Vocabulary

Study these new words. Learning the meanings of these words is a good study habit and will improve your understanding of this LIFEPAC.

bronze (bronz). A reddish-brown metal made by melting together copper and tin.

disobedient (dis' u bē' dē unt). Not willing to obey.

disobey (dis' u bā'). To fail to obey.

doer (dü' ur). Person who does something.

long-suffering (lông' suf' ur ing). Patient.

Nicodemus (nik' ō dē' mus). A ruler of the Jews.

obedient (ō bē' dē unt). Willing to obey.

Pronunciation Key: hat, āge, cãre, fär; let, ēqual, tėrm; it, īce; hot, ōpen, ôrder; oil; out; cup, pu̇t, rüle; child; long; thin; /ŦH/ for then; /zh/ for measure; /u/ or /ə/ represents /a/ in about, /e/ in taken, /i/ in pencil, /o/ in lemon, and /u/ in circus.

Be Born into God's Family

Read 1 Peter 2:2;
John 3:1–15;
Numbers 21:5–9
and John 1:12.

When Uncle Gerald came to visit, Linda and Leonard had many questions. Linda asked the first question. "God says (First Peter 2:2), 'As newborn babes, desire the sincere milk of the word, that ye may grow thereby.' What does *newborn babes* mean?"

Uncle Gerald answered, "God teaches that we need a new life in Him. He calls it 'being born again.'"

Then Uncle Gerald told the children about a man named **Nicodemus** (John 3:1–13). He was a ruler of the Jews. He came to see Jesus at night. Jesus told him about being born again. Nicodemus didn't understand. He asked how an old man could be born again. Jesus told him the second birth was a spiritual birth.

Our physical selves were born into an earthly family. Our spiritual selves need to be born into a heavenly family. The heavenly family is the family of God. We are born into God's family when the Holy Spirit cleanses us from sin and Jesus puts His life in us.

Then Jesus told Nicodemus a story from the history of the Israelites. A long time ago the children of Israel had **disobeyed** God and Moses (Numbers 21:5–9). God sent fiery serpents among the people. The serpents bit the people. Many died.

The people came crying to Moses. The people told Moses they had sinned. They told him what they had done. The people asked Moses to pray for them. They wanted him to ask that the serpents be removed. Moses prayed for them.

| Nicodemus meets Jesus

God told Moses what to do. God said to make a fiery serpent. Moses was to lift it up on a pole. When anyone was bitten, he could look at the serpent and he would live.

Moses made a **bronze** serpent. He put it on a pole. Those who were bitten and looked at the bronze serpent, did not die. They got better and lived.

Jesus told Nicodemus that Jesus Himself would be lifted up on a Cross. Those who would look to Him as "the Lamb of God" who can take away sin, would live (John 3:14 and 15).

Peter wrote about this same thing in one of his letters in the New Testament (1 Peter 2:24), "Who his own self bare our sins in his own body on the tree, that we, being dead to sins, should live unto righteousness: by whose stripes ye were healed."

Linda said, "I know I've sinned. I believe Jesus died to take away my sin. I now receive the life of God, which is God's gift to me. I believe the Holy Spirit lives in my heart."

Leonard also was born into God's family.

Have you been born into God's family?

 Do these activities. Here's a message from the Bible written in Morse code. Use the Morse code to find the message.

International Morse Code

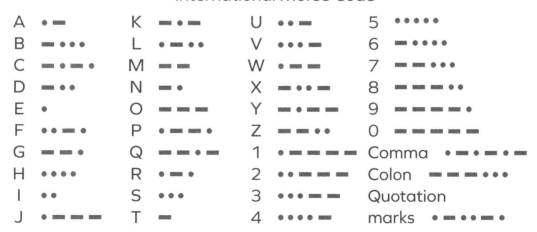

2.1   Write the correct alphabet letter on the line above the code.

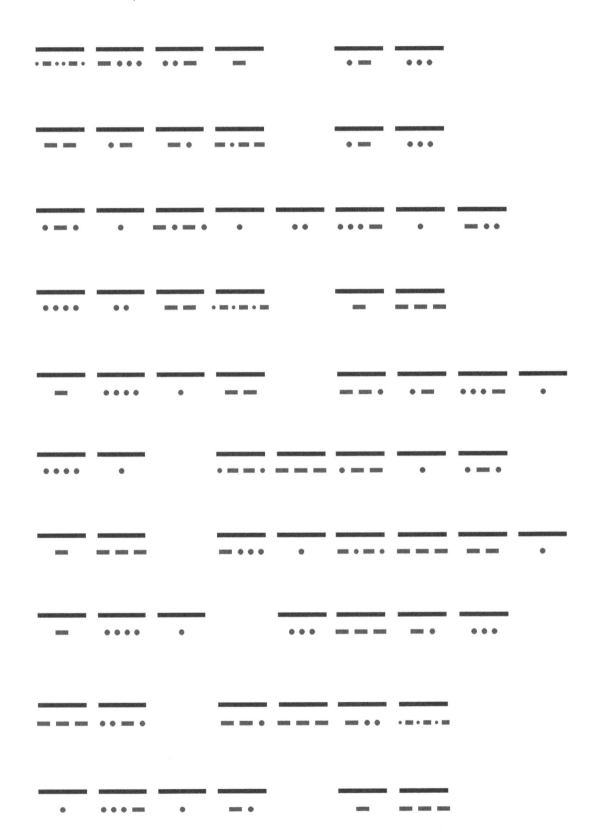

2.2 Write the Bible verse, John 1:12, on these lines.

_____

_____

_____

_____

_____

_____

_____

_____

Memorize John 1:12.
Say it from memory to a teacher.

Teacher check:

Initials _____

Date _____

Grow as God's Child

Read 1 Peter 2:2 and James 1:22-24.

"Now I understand," Linda said one day. "I remember when Laurie was born. She needed her bottle of milk. She cried to let Mother know when she was hungry. Milk helped her to grow. I'm like that in God's family now," Linda said. "My milk is God's Word."

"Could we read the Bible now, Uncle Gerald?" Leonard asked.

"That's a good idea. Let's look at what God says about His Word (James 1:22 through 24). 'But be ye doers of the word, and not hearers only, deceiving your own selves. For if any be a hearer of the word, and not a doer, he is like unto a man beholding his natural face in a glass:

For he beholdeth himself, and goeth his way, and straightway forgetteth what manner of man he was.'"

"I want to be a **doer** of what God says. I want to be clean from sin," Linda said.

"Peter was a doer of God's Word, wasn't he, Uncle Gerald? Remember the time when he followed Jesus? When Jesus told him to let down the net, Peter obeyed. I remember. Peter said (Luke 5:5), 'Master, we have toiled all the night, and have taken nothing: nevertheless at thy word I will let down the net.'"

Uncle Gerald reminded the children that most of the time Peter was **obedient**,

| The One Who Only Hears God's Word

| The One Who Does God's Word

but sometimes he was **disobedient**. God says that Christians still sin. He tells us what to do when we sin. God says (1 John 1:9), "If we confess our sins, he is faithful and just to forgive us our sins, and to cleanse us from all unrighteousness."

"What does *confess* mean, Uncle Gerald?" Linda asked.

"Confess means to tell God about your sin," Uncle Gerald said.

"A Christian can be cleansed from sin by doing two things, can't he?" Leonard asked. "First, obey God. Second, confess when you disobey."

"I've really enjoyed studying God's Word," Linda said.

Do this puzzle activity.

2.3   Read the clues to the crossword puzzle.
Fill in the blanks in the puzzle.

Down

1.   What God does with sin

4.   What Jesus did on the Cross for our sins

5.   Made a bronze serpent

Across

2.   What we should do with sin

3.   Asked about the new birth

2.4   On these lines write the words from the puzzle followed by their clues.

	Word	Clue
1.	_____	_____
2.	_____	_____
3.	_____	_____
4.	_____	_____
5.	_____	_____

Be Fruitful Through the Spirit

Read Galatians 5:22 and 5:23; John 13:35; 1 John 5:14; 2 Peter 3:9 and Luke 15:10.

"Linda," said Leonard, "I just found something very interesting in Galatians 5:22 and 23. Listen.

'But the fruit of the Spirit is love, joy, peace, longsuffering, gentleness, goodness, faith, meekness, temperance: against such there is no law.' I guess we need all this fruit. Let's think about each word."

"*Love.* When I first read Jesus' words, 'Love your enemies,' I didn't think I could do it," Linda said. "But I prayed for them as Jesus said to do, and God gave me a love for them."

"We see love in our church, too," Leonard added. "It reminds me of Jesus' words in John 13:35, 'By this shall all men know that ye are my disciples, if ye have love one to another.'"

"*Joy.* I've read about Christians who sang through very hard times. God can really cause a Christian to have joy," Linda said.

"If you have God, how could you be without joy?" Leonard asked.

"I don't know," Linda said. "Maybe some people forget God is always with them."

"*Peace.* Isn't it good that we don't have to be worried about things anymore?" Leonard said.

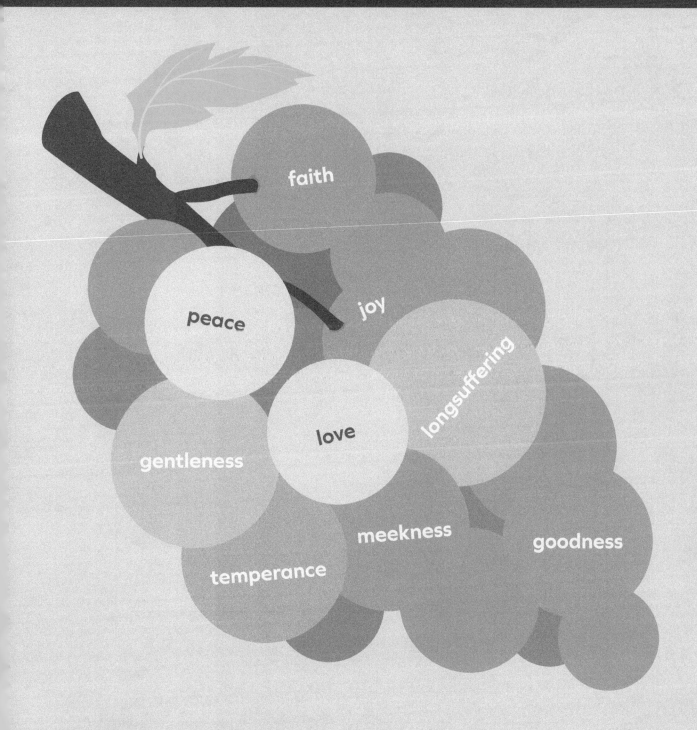

"Longsuffering. That's another word for patience, isn't it?" Linda asked.

"That's right." Leonard answered.

"And I've noticed you have been more patient with Laurie."

"Thanks, Leonard. God is patient with me," Linda said.

"Let's stop with four of them. I just can't take in anymore for a while," Leonard said.

Do these activities.

2.5   Leonard made a puzzle for Linda. She was to look for the "fruit of the Spirit."
Can you help her find them?

Draw a line around the words that name the "fruit of the Spirit."

T	H	E	F	R	U	I	T	O	F	T	H	E	S	P
H	O	L	A	I	N	K	R	W	A	R	O	V	O	E
A	N	O	I	G	M	I	T	R	U	S	J	E	B	A
G	E	N	T	L	E	N	E	S	S	O	O	B	E	C
O	B	G	H	O	E	D	M	E	R	C	Y	E	Y	E
O	K	S	O	V	K	N	P	O	W	E	R	I	G	H
D	I	U	N	E	N	E	E	B	I	V	I	M	O	O
N	N	F	O	V	E	S	R	E	S	E	G	N	D	L
E	D	F	U	E	S	S	A	D	D	R	H	O	L	Y
S	N	E	R	I	S	O	N	C	O	N	F	I	D	E
S	G	R	A	C	E	B	C	O	M	P	A	S	S	I
O	L	I	G	H	T	R	E	N	A	R	S	A	A	M
B	O	N	O	A	R	I	G	F	J	A	S	N	N	M
E	R	G	D	R	U	G	R	I	E	I	U	C	C	O

2.6   List the names of the "fruit of the Spirit" on the lines.

a. _____   b. _____

c. _____   d. _____

e. _____   f. _____

g. _____   h. _____

i. _____

2.7   Write the place in the Bible where the "fruit of the Spirit" is listed.

_____

As the Holy Spirit works in your life to make you like Christ, God will provide times for you to tell others what Christ has done for you.

If you love your enemies, they will wonder why. You will be able to tell them that God loves them.

One teacher was always happy. Her students noticed this. They asked her why she was always happy. She was able to tell them what Jesus had done for her.

| Jesus and his followers

One girl was sick. She asked her pastor what she could do to bring others to Jesus. He encouraged her to pray for those she knew who didn't know Jesus. She made a list of people to pray for. Everyone on this list came to Jesus. She made another list. The last person on that list came to Jesus the day the girl died. In a short time twenty-nine people came to Jesus.

God does answer prayer for those who need Jesus. In God's Word we read (First John 5:14), "And this is the confidence that we have in him, that, if we ask anything according to his will, he heareth us."

We know it is God's will for people to become Christians. In Second Peter 3:9 we read, "The Lord is...not willing that any should perish, but that all should come to repentance."

Jesus said (Luke 15:10), "...there is joy in the presence of the angels of God over one sinner that repenteth."

There is no greater joy for the Christian than to see someone come to Jesus. When you bring someone to Jesus, you cause joy in Heaven.

As you live for God, you may see many come to Jesus and begin to live for Him too.

Practice using suffixes.

2.8 **Add the suffixes** *-ed* **and** *-ing* **to the following root words**. Remember to drop the final *e* when it is silent before adding a suffix that begins with a vowel. The suffix *-ed* cannot be added to two of the root words. These words are irregular. See if you can remember them.

Root Word	-ed Ending	-ing Ending
a. come	a. _____	b. _____
b. complete	a. _____	b. _____
c. decide	a. _____	b. _____
d. excite	a. _____	b. _____
e. give	a. _____	b. _____
f. introduce	a. _____	b. _____
g. invite	a. _____	b. _____
h. live	a. _____	b. _____
i. name	a. _____	b. _____
j. receive	a. _____	b. _____

Pray for someone.

2.9   Make a list of people you would like to see come to Jesus.
Write the date you begin to pray for them.
Write the date they come to Jesus. You may want to
write this information on another piece of paper and put
it in your Bible. The note will remind you to pray for them.

I'm praying for	I began to pray on	They came to Jesus on
_____	_____	_____
_____	_____	_____
_____	_____	_____
_____	_____	_____
_____	_____	_____

✔ **Teacher check:**

Initials _____   Date _____

**Before you take this last Self Test, you may want to do one or more of these
self checks.**

1. _____   Read the objectives. See if you can do them.
2. _____   Restudy the material related to any objectives that you cannot do.
3. _____   Use the **SQ3R** study procedure to review the material:
    a. **S**can the sections.
    b. **Q**uestion yourself.
    c. **R**ead to answer your questions.
    d. **R**ecite the answers to yourself.
    e. **R**eview areas you did not understand.
4. _____   Review all vocabulary, activities, and Self Tests, writing a correct answer
    for every wrong answer.

SELF TEST 2

Complete these statements (each answer counts 4 points).

2.01   Jesus trained _____ disciples.

2.02   Jesus taught that you should love your _____ .

2.03   God says a Christian should confess his _____ .

2.04   We should be _____ of God's Word.

2.05   Nicodemus was a _____ .

Answer these questions (each answer counts 4 points).

2.06   What does *sin* mean? _____

2.07   What is the result of sin? _____

2.08   What story did Jesus tell to explain the new birth?

_____

_____

2.09   What does God do when a Christian confesses his sin?

a. _____   b. _____

2.010 What does the word *confess* mean? _____

2.011 After Jesus arose from the dead, what did He want Peter to do?

_____

_____

2.012 How can a Christian have a cleansed heart?

a. _____   b. _____

2.013 How did Jesus say others would know that you are His disciples?

_____

_____

2.014 Why did Peter start to sink in the water? _____

_____

2.015   What are some names of the "fruit of the Spirit" that you studied in this section?

a. _____   b. _____

c. _____   d. _____

e. _____

2.016   What does longsuffering mean? _____

Add the suffixes -ed **and** -ing **to these words** (each answer counts 1 point).
Note: two words are irregular.

Root Word	-ed Ending	-ing Ending
2.017 complete	_____	_____
2.018 love	_____	_____
2.019 give	_____	_____
2.020 deceive	_____	_____
2.021 produce	_____	_____
2.022 come	_____	_____

Teacher check: Initials _____   80
Score _____   Date _____   / 100

Before you take the LIFEPAC Test, you may want to do one or more of these self checks.

1. _____ Read the objectives. See if you can do them.
2. _____ Restudy the material related to any objectives that you cannot do.
3. _____ Use the **SQ3R** study procedure to review the material.
4. _____ Review activities, Self Tests, and LIFEPAC vocabulary words.
5. _____ Restudy areas of weakness indicated by the last Self Test.

NOTES

NOTES